MW01040253

Parakeets : A Complete Parakeet Owners Guide

What Parakeets Eat, Breeding Parakeets, Training And Caring For Them

By: Alan McDaniel

ISBN-13: 978-1478135906

Publishers Notes

BINDERS PUBLISHING LLC

Disclaimer

This publication is intended to provide helpful and informative material. It is not intended to diagnose, treat, cure, or prevent any health problem or condition, nor is intended to replace the advice of a physician. No action should be taken solely on the contents of this book. Always consult your physician or qualified health-care professional on any matters regarding your health and before adopting any suggestions in this book or drawing inferences from it.

The author and publisher specifically disclaim all responsibility for any liability, loss or risk, personal or otherwise, which is incurred as a consequence, directly or indirectly, from the use or application of any contents of this book.

Any and all product names referenced within this book are the trademarks of their respective owners. None of these owners have sponsored, authorized, endorsed, or approved this book.

Always read all information provided by the manufacturers' product labels before using their products. The author and publisher are not responsible for claims made by manufacturers.

The statements made in this book have not been evaluated by the Food and Drug Administration.

Binders Publishing LLC
7950 NW 53rd Street
Miami,
FL 33166

Alan McDaniel

Kindle Edition 2012

BINDERS PUBLISHING PRESS is a trademark of Binders Publishing LLC.

For information about special discounts for bulk purchases, please contact Binders Publishing Sales Department at 954-379-7796 or publishing@binderspublishing.com

Designed by Colin WF Scott

Manufactured in the United States of America

ISBN-13: 978-1478135906

Alan McDaniel

Table of Contents

Dedication

I dedicate this book to all the bird lovers out there like me. I love my pet Parakeet and he is so much a part of my family like how your bird is take care of them and they will love you for it.

CHAPTER 1- FACTS ABOUT PARAKEETS : A FEW FACTS ABOUT THIS BIRD EVERY OWNER SHOULD KNOW

The term parakeet is used for any of a huge number of species of unrelated small or medium parrots and these parrots usually have tail feathers that are long. There is also the term Grass Parakeet or Grasskeet which is used in reference to many small Australian parakeets ta are the natives of such grasslands as Princess Parrot and Neophema. In addition, there are also the rosellas again from Australia.

The parakeets from Africa include the ring necked parakeets which are a species of the psittacula genus and these are indigenous to both Asia and Africa. There are popular pets but have also become wild in a number of cities. These are however different from the ring neck parakeets that are from Australia.

The term conure is used in aviculture in reference t small to medium parakeets of the genera Aratinga Pyrrhura, and there are also some other genere that comes from the tribe of Arini and these are mostly found in South America. There are other species from South America such as the Brotogeris, the Monk as well as the short-tailed lineolated parakeets.

There are some species of parrots they are referred to as either a parakeet or a parrot, specifically the parakeets that are larger. The Psittacula eupatria is one of the largest species of parakeets there is. There are a number of species of parakeets that are being raised and then commercially sold as pets and the Budgerigar is usually the commonest species that is used in this regard.

Parakeets, the Budgeries, Keets or Budgies as they are sometimes called are best raised in groups. However, they will be just fine if you choose to raise them as a pair. They thrive better in groups due to the fact that when they hear other parakeets they are encouraged to breed and this speaks to the greater success that breeding them in groups usually have. Breeders often times prefer to breed them in pairs though, simply because in that way they are able to know who parented them.

Some conure species that are very familiar are the black hooded parakeets or the ones that are otherwise known as Nanday Conure, and there is also the mitred Conure. The variety of parakeets in existence are very many and there are both species as well as sub species. They can be small, medium sized as well as large parakeets. They grow to sizes that range between approximately seven inches to about eighteen inches lengthwise. They have very bright and beautiful colors. However, the exact range of their coloring is determined by the type of parakeets and where they are from. Their colors range from blues, greens, oranges, yellows and reds, among a number of other colors. The strict definition of the word parakeet is long tail and they usually have bodies that are slender and tails feathers that are tapered and long. Their upper bills are hooked and they use them for climbing, digging as well as for holding things in their mouth. They also peel fruits, break seeds and chew with their beaks.

A number of parakeets have a cere that is unfeathered that is at the top of their beak and that goes around their nostrils. The coloration that is on the cere of some parakeets like the Budgerigar is quite different for the male than it is for the females and this makes it very easy for you to make the differentiation between the two.

Chapter 2- What Parakeets Eat : Feeding Parakeets Requires This Type Of Knowledge

Many parakeets eat some of the parts of will bird food and these comprise of a number of seeds to include sunflower seeds and these are not included in the seed mix for parakeets often times. These wild seeds are not toxic but some unhealthy contents may be contained in them and a small number of parakeets may actually die from eating them. This is not a long term diet for parakeets as there may be seeds that are high in fat; as in the sunflower seeds and this can cause health issues as the bird gets older. This is largely due to the fact that these wild bird foods are not placed under the rating standard that parakeet feed is placed under, and these seeds have to comprise of seeds that still have the ability to sprout.

The experts recommend that you stick to pet-grade quality seeds for your parakeets. In addition, they need a diet than is more diverse than only seeds, they need vegetables, bee pollen as well as fruits and these are usually in the feed mixes for parakeets.

As their base diet, you should start them off with parakeet seed mix that are of good quality, organic ones if that is possible. Dr. Harvey's Bird Food Mixes are great as they do not have any kinds of additives that are not good for the parakeets and that are usually in the commercial mixes. Dr. Harvey's bird food mixes usually comprise of veggies, greens or herbs and dried fruits, the nourishing ingredients that are not usually in the bird mixes that are accessible commercially. Harrison's is also a good quality formulated diet for parakeets and this is commonly recommended by veterinarians.

The vegetables and fruits are very important to a parakeet's diet, especially the ones that are being bred as pets. They should get grapes and apples as well as vegetables such as chickweed, carrots, peas, spinach, field lettuce, dandelions, endives, watercress, sweet potatoes as well as corn on the cob. If you are not able to get fresh veggies you can feed them human baby food with vegetables and fruits such as Gerber baby foods.

Dried fruits are also workable as well. They can eat them as is or you can sometimes moisten them so that they will be rehydrated. You should be mindful of the fact that some manufacturers will have additives in these dried fruits and vegetables in order for them to be more colorful and more visually appealing. As such, you should stick to purchasing those dried fruits that do not have sulfur dioxide since the preservative usually increases picking caused by allergies, aggressiveness as well as hyperactivity. You should never feed your parakeets avocado, chocolate, drinks that are caffeinated, alcohol or the pits of fruits.

CHAPTER 3- BREEDING PARAKEETS : IF YOU WANT TO BREED PARAKEETS THEN THIS IS A MUST READ

When you are breeding parakeets you will need to make sure that the breeding parakeets as well as their babies are healthy. This includes ensuring that the pair you are about to breed are not related, are at least one year old and are also free from birth defects as well as from disease.

The cage that is required for a pair of parakeets that you will be breeding is a minimum of 20"x20"x20". In addition, it should have a nest box that is made of wood that is 12" x 12" at least. There are some breeders of parakeets that put inserts made of wood into the bottom of the nest boxes so that they can prevent the birds from having splay legs. However, when this is done you will have to have the correct nesting material like pine shavings.

Due to the fact that parakeets are hookbills they must be fed a diet that varies and that comprise of a lot of fruits and vegetables as mentioned before as well as pellets that are of high quality and different seeds. When you are breeding a pair of parakeets then they should be getting a calcium and cuttlebone supplement so as to make sure that their eggs are developed properly as well as to help the hen to recover the nutrients that they lost when they are making their eggs.

With respect to the laying of their eggs, the female parakeets' eggs will be laid comparatively soon after they have mated. It is common for parakeets as it is with other kinds of birds, to lay an egg a day until all the eggs are laid. Albeit there can be a variation, they normally lay between four and eight eggs in every clutch. The incubation time on average for parakeet eggs is usually between seventeen and twenty days but can go a few days in either direction and this will be fine.

If you are taming the parakeets as pets, then breeders often times let the parents raise their own chicks until the time comes for them to be weaned. However, the breeder will usually handle them sometimes so that they can become accustomed to the hands of human beings. A majority of baby chicks are weaned by they are six weeks old and then they can e taken from their parents and can now interact with human beings on their own.

CHAPTER 4- PARAKEETS TRAINING : CAN PARAKEETS TALK, THIS CHAPTER WILL TELL YOU HOW TO MAKE YOURS CHAT

In training a parakeet it is important for you to concentrate on repetition, bonding as well as on their personality. They can learn very quickly if they are thought in the right way. Repeating words and phrases are very important to the training process, just in the same way as it is in teaching human beings how to read.

It has been found that birds learn best in the morning as this is the time that their minds are fresh and prepared to take in new information. One way to teach your bird is to cover their cage and talk to them for an half an hour before removing the cover every morning. Then repeat the same phrases in a voice that is clear, slow and loud.

They are very good with the letters T and K so hello is not very easy for them, but cutie would be a breeze. They have a tendency to talk very fast as well as to mumble, as such, talking to them slowly will help them to sound a little more normal when they start to repeat what you say to them.

You will have to exercise patience however and then in time they will start responding to you. As soon as they begin to learn to repeat what you say then they will learn more quickly as you go along. You should also tape your voice so that the parakeet can hear it while you are away, but what happens sometimes when this is done is that they will tend towards talking only when you are not there. There are parakeets that can learn words after as short as 2 months while others can learn to talk by 6 months' time.

Other tips for teaching your parakeet how to talk include buying the bird when they are young, encouraging bonding between you and the bird very early with the offer of a hand and then letting them sit on your shoulder. In addition, you should make sure you stay away from using words that are offensive as those are the words that will be repeated by your parakeet.

Chapter 5- Types Of Parakeets : The Different Types And Which One May Be Right For You

As mentioned previously, there are a number of types of parakeets, the following are a much more exhaustive list of parakeets and where they come from. There are more than thirty species of parakeets in Australia alone. The exotic Australian parakeets are inclusive of:

Regent Parakeet

Elegant Parakeet

The parakeet with the blue wings

Turquoise Parakeet

Princess of Wales

The Parakeet with the Red rump

The Stanley Parakeet

The Mulga Parakeet

Bourke's Parakeet

The paraeets with the chest

The Parakeet with the Red wings

Red capped Parakeet

Australian King Parakeet

Superb Parakeet

Mallee Ring neck Parakeet

Port Lincoln Parakeet

There are also 5 of the 6 species of Rosellas come from Australia. Some of these Australian Rosella are the Pennant's, the Golden-manteled or Earstern Rosella as well as the pale headed rosella.

There are also many parakeets that come from Asia. Asia's exotic parakeets have a number of unique characteristics. They can have a very diverse kind of qualities as it relates to them being raised as pets and this can vary from one bird to the other. There will be those who will be very friendly and will be easy to train how to speak, while on the other hand, there are others who may not be that way. Generally, many of these parakeets are not as lively as the smaller parrots but this does not mean that they do not make very good pets as well. Other Asian parakeets are inclusive of:

Slaty headed Parakeet

Plum-headed Parakeet

Alexandrine Parakeet

Intermediate Parakeet or Rothschild's Parakeet

Ring neck parakeet or the Indian Ring neck Parakeet

The parakeet with the mustach

Derbyan Parakeet

Newton Parakeet

Blossom headed Parakeet

Emerald collared Parakeet

Blyth's Parakeet

The Long tailed Parakeet, also referred to as Malayan Red cheeked Parakeet and Pink cheeked Parakeets

Seychelles Parakeets

Mauritius Parakeet

Malabar Parakeet

The parakeets that hail from New Zealand include their 3 exotic species as well as a few subspecies. The islands that neighbor them also have a number of species of parakeets as well. The parakeets from New Zealand also include the yellow-fronted parakeet or as they are sometimes referred to as yellow-crowned parakeets, the Malherbe's parakeet as well as the critically endangered species, the Orange-fronted parakeets. There are also the red-fronted parakeets also known as the Kakariki parakeets and the Fore's yellow-fronted parakeets.

There are also those parakeets that are indigenous to both South America as well as Central America. Those exotic parakeets that come from South America and Central America usually have colorings that are not as strong as the parakeets that come from Australia but they are still very beautiful birds that can make very good pets as well. Some of the more familiar parakeets from these areas are the Barred Parakeets, the Canary-winged Parakeets, the Grey-cheeked Parakeets, the Quaker parakeet or monk parakeets, the Tui Parakeet as well as the Orange chinned Parakeets.

Parakeets are quite intelligent birds and each of the species of these parakeets have their own different calls and some being able to mimic all the sounds they are hearing around them. There are pet parakeets that have been known to live longer than those that live in the wild. The life span that is average for all parakeets is not necessarily known, however for small parakeets such as the Budgie.

Parakeets or the Budgerigar, the Bourke's Parakeet as well as the Elegant Parakeets can live up to ten years of age. The bigger parakeets like the Ring neck parakeets and the regent parakeet can live up to the age of twenty five.

CHAPTER 6- CAGES FOR PARAKEETS : THIS IS AS IMPORTANT AS WHAT YOU FEED THE BIRD

When parakeets are in the wild they really enjoy flying around. As such, they need to have enough room in order for them to be healthy and happy in their bird cage. What this means is that the bigger the cage is then the better it will be for them. For a pair of parakeets that are medium in size, you will need to get them a bird cage that is thirty nine inches times twenty inches by thirty two inches. Since they like to climb almost as much as they like to fly, the vertical space is as important as the horizontal space.

In addition to the foregoing, they do not like the cold and so it is imperative that you keep their cages away from the doors and the windows. Strong smells such as those coming from the kitchens and the bathrooms are not something they like either and therefore they should be kept as far away from them as possible. They have a requirement of sixty to seventy percent level of humidity. What this means is that in areas that is dry and in the winter time when the humidity level in a number of areas are quite low, then you may need a humidifier for the area where the bird cage is being kept.

There should be a number of bird perches in the bird cages, with some higher up in the cage and others being placed in position for the bird food dishes and the waterer. There should also be a cuttle bone in the cages so that their beak can be kept in shape and to provide them the additional calcium. Concrete perches and Lava stones should also be placed in the bird cage and you can also place branches in the cage as well since they enjoy chewing on branches or different types. They are also in love with bird toys so you can place thick hemp lengths of ropes that will work as very god gnawing toys for them. They also enjoy bird cage ladders and bird swings and therefore these can be something else that can be placed inside their cages. You should stay away from placing toys in their cages that can be harmful to them though, such as those toys that have parts that are breakable or that come with strings that are thin.

Whatever you decide to put inside the bird cage for your parakeet to keep them active and entertained, you just need to ensure that are safe and will not end up harming them. Do not fill it with too many things though, as remember that they need the room to both climb and to fly around in their cage. You can always look at websites in order to find the websites with the right dimensions for your parakeets. These bird cages can also be found in bird stores as well. You can find many different types of bird cages as varying different prices to house your parakeets and do so very comfortably.

CHAPTER 7- RING NECKED PARAKEETS : WHY WE ALWAYS RECOMMEND THIS TYPE

The Latin name for ring necked parakeets is Psittacula krameri. The ring necked parakeet is actually the only naturalized parakeet in the United Kingdom. It is a large bird and has a long tail and is colored in green with a red beak as well as a black and pink ring that is around its neck and face. When t is flying it has wings that are pointed, and their long tails make them very steady and direct. You will be able to find these birds mostly in the southern-eastern end of England; specifically in Kent, Sussex and Surrey.

They can be seen all year round and they eat nuts, fruits, seeds and berries. There are approximately four thousand, three hundred adult birds in the UK. There is usually the Europe UK breeding which refers to the number of pairs of ring necked parakeets that are been bred annually, the UK passage speaks to the number of individual birds that pass through as they migrate in the spring and/or in the autumn and the UK wintering is in reference to the number of these birds that are present from October until March.

These types of parakeets are initially from southern Asia as well as from Africa and they are usually kept as birds that are caged. There are some ring necked parakeets that escaped and by the 1970s they started to breed in south eastern England and you can find their biggest population in Esher, in Surrey and the roost can hold up to approximately seven thousand birds.

The feathers of both sexes of these parakeets is bright emerald green, their bills are hooked and crimson in color as they have very long blue-green tails with greenish-grey legs. You can make the differentiation between the males and the females of the species by the black and pink ring around the necks of the males, as well as their blue napes. The young females are just like the older females, except that they are a little more yellow and have a tail that is shorter.

The ring necked parakeets are quite noisy creatures who have a call that is very shrill and screeching. They eat berries, fruits, seeds, nectar and flowers. The British birds also add wild bird seeds and meats such as meat from bones and bacon rind to their diets. These birds were first bred in 1969 were they usually nested in a hole of a tree and made from feathers as well as from wooden debris. They lay smooth, non-glossy white eggs that are about 30 mm by 23 mm in size and the females hatch their eggs themselves. When the young birds are hatched, both parents feed them.

These parakeets thrive in the south east of England because of the lack of predators and their mild winters. They are now moving to the far northern areas such as Leeds and Sheffield now as well. These parakeets make very good pets which is why they are such popular pets in the United Kingdom as well as in other countries around the world.

ABOUT THE AUTHOR

Alan McDaniel grew up deathly afraid of birds since one fateful day in the park when he was four years old and a pigeon flew down and took the popcorn he was eating right out of his hands and flew away. He stayed far away from all birds from that day onwards. Well at least until that day he went to the zoo and saw the ring-necked parakeets and was awe-struck by their beautiful colors and the fact that they could actually speak. He surprised his dad by asking him if he could go closer t to bird cage and actually touch the bird. He was tentative at first but after the first touch of those smooth, beautiful feathers, he was completely in love and his love affair led him to breed them as well as to have them as pets.

He travels all over the world to find them and photograph them and has a collection of wonderful pictures in a studio that is reserved just for developing and hanging his pictures of his beloved parakeets. Albeit he is not obsessed enough to deserve the "bird man" nickname he has gotten, he is certainly in awe of parakeets so much so that he can tell you anything you wish to now about and he could do this even in his sleep. The birds love him as much as he loves them and even the ones he gives away to loving homes, he still see them as his babies and keep track of them no matter how far away from him they end up having their home.

Kindle Edition 2012

BINDERS PUBLISHING PRESS is a trademark of Binders Publishing LLC.

For information about special discounts for bulk purchases, please contact Binders Publishing Sales Department at 954-379-7796 or publishing@binderspublishing.com

Designed by Colin WF Scott

Manufactured in the United States of America

ISBN-13: 978-1478135906

77524419R00015

Made in the USA
Columbia, SC
22 September 2017